AZAI'S
A-B-C AFFIRMATIONS

Khadijahr.wilson@yahoo.com

Copyright © 2020 Khadijah Wilson

Azai's ABC Affirmations

We can start off our days in such a rush getting ready for work and school that we forget to take a moment to love ourselves. Every morning I say my daughter's affirmations to her to start the day with positivity. I want other parents to be able to speak life into their children to be sure that their day is filled with love, peace, and happiness. You can start saying these to them while they are young and then they will be able to say it along with you as they grow up. I believe that speaking these affirmations will help with self-love to build more confidence and also great for bonding. I hope that you enjoy this book!

Azai's ABC Affirmations

I created my daughter's affirmations
before she was born by using her name
as a guide.

The meaning of Azai is strength.

Here are Baby Azai's affirmations:

**I AM AZAI. I AM STRONG.
I AM AMAZING.
I AM ZEN.
I AM AMBITIOUS.
I AM INTELLIGENT.
I AM STRONG. I AM AZAI.
I AM THAT I AM.**

Now you and your baby can create your own affirmations as well. You may start with using a word that starts with the letters that spells out their name. Here are some words A-Z to get you started!

I AM ARTISTIC.

I AM AWESOME.

I AM BRILLIANT.
I AM BEAUTIFUL.

C

I AM CREATIVE.

I AM CONFIDENT.

D

I AM DETERMINED.

I AM DYNAMIC.

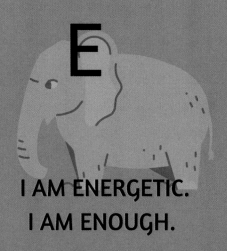

E

I AM ENERGETIC.

I AM ENOUGH.

F

I AM FORGIVING.

I AM FUN.

G

I AM GRATEFUL.
I AM GENEROUS.

H

I AM HAPPY.

I AM HANDSOME.

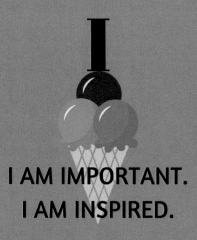

I AM IMPORTANT.
I AM INSPIRED.

I AM JOYFUL.
I AM JOLLY.

K

I AM KIND-HEARTED.
I AM KNOWLEDGEABLE.

I AM LOVED.
I AM A LEADER.

M

I AM MOTIVATED.
I AM MAGICAL.

I AM NICE.
I AM NATURAL.

O

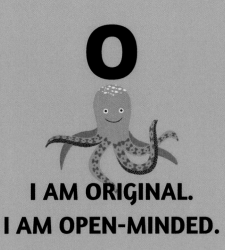

I AM ORIGINAL.

I AM OPEN-MINDED.

P

I AM POSITIVE.
I AM PASSIONATE.

I AM A QUEEN.
I AM QUIRKY.

I AM RESPECTFUL.
I AM RESPONSIBLE.

S

I AM SINCERE.
I AM SMART.

T

I AM THOUGHTFUL.
I AM TRUSTWORTHY.

I AM UNIQUE.
I AM UNDERSTANDING.

I AM VALUABLE.
I AM VICTORIOUS.

W

I AM WISE.

I AM WONDERFUL.

X

I AM eXTRAORDINARY.

I AM eXCELLENT.

Y

I AM YOUTHFUL.

I AM ZEN.

Now you can use this space to
write your affirmations!

Be sure to start with **I AM...**

Azai's ABC Affirmations

I truly hope that you
and your little one
enjoyed this book and
your time together.
Remember you are
AMAZING just the way
YOU are!

Made in the USA
Columbia, SC
05 December 2022

72564380R00020